THE NEW BEST SHERYL CROW FOR GUITAR

C000296378

Arranged by LOUIS MARTINEZ

Project Manager: COLGAN BRYAN
Book Design: JOSEPH KLUCAR
Photography: ROBERTO SANTOS

WARNER BROS. PUBLICATIONS - THE GLOBAL LEADER IN PRINT
USA: 15800 NW 48th Avenue, Miami, FL 33014

WARNER/CHAPPELL MUSIC

CANADA: 85 SCARSDALE ROAD, SUITE 101
DON MILLS, ONTARIO, M3B 2R2
SCANDINAVIA: P.O. BOX 533, VENDEVAGEN 85 B
S-182 15, DANDERYD, SWEDEN
AUSTRALIA: P.O. BOX 353
3 TALAVERA ROAD, NORTH RYDE N.S.W. 2113

NUOVA CARISCH

ITALY: VIA M.F. QUINTILIANO 40
20138 MILANO
SPAIN: MAGALLANES, 25
28015 MADRID

INTERNATIONAL MUSIC PUBLICATIONS LIMITED

ENGLAND: SOUTHEND ROAD,
WOODFORD GREEN, ESSEX IG8 8HN
FRANCE: 25 RUE DE HAUTEVILLE, 75010 PARIS
GERMANY: MARSTALLISTR. 8, D-80539 MUNCHEN
DENMARK: DANMUSIK, VOGNMAGERGADE 7
DK 1120 KOBENHAVNK

GUITAR TAB GLOSSARY **

TABLATURE EXPLANATION

READING TABLATURE: Tablature illustrates the six strings of the guitar. Notes and chords are indicated by the placement of fret numbers on a given string(s).

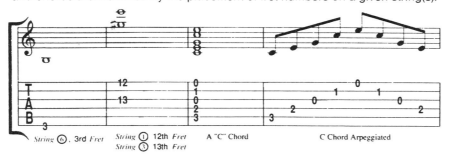

String ⑥, 3rd Fret   *String ① 12th Fret*   A "C" Chord   C Chord Arpeggiated
                    String ③ 13th Fret

BENDING NOTES

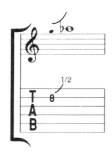

HALF STEP: Play the note and bend string one half step.*

WHOLE STEP: Play the note and bend string one whole step.

PREBEND AND RELEASE: Bend the string, play it, then release to the original note.

RHYTHM SLASHES

STRUM INDICA-TIONS: Strum with indicated rhythm. The chord voicings are found on the first page of the transcription underneath the song title.

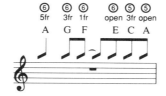

INDICATING SINGLE NOTES USING RHYTHM SLASHES: Very often single notes are incorporated into a rhythm part. The note name is indicated above the rhythm slash with a fret number and a string indication.

*A half step is the smallest interval in Western music; it is equal to one fret. A whole step equals two frets.

**By Kenn Chipkin and Aaron Stang

ARTICULATIONS

HAMMER ON: Play lower note, then "hammer on" to higher note with another finger. Only the first note is attacked.

PULL OFF: Play higher note, then "pull off" to lower note with another finger. Only the first note is attacked.

LEGATO SLIDE: Play note and slide to the following note. (Only first note is attacked).

PALM MUTE: The note or notes are muted by the palm of the pick hand by lightly touching the string(s) near the bridge.

ACCENT: Notes or chords are to be played with added emphasis.

DOWN STROKES AND UPSTROKES: Notes or chords are to be played with either a downstroke (⊓ ·) or upstroke (∨) of the pick.

CONTENTS

ALL I WANNA DO 4

CAN'T CRY ANYMORE 10

A CHANGE WOULD DO YOU GOOD 14

EVERYDAY IS A WINDING ROAD 18

HARD TO MAKE A STAND 24

IF IT MAKES YOU HAPPY 28

LEAVING LAS VEGAS 33

LOVE IS A GOOD THING 38

MAYBE ANGELS 44

THE NA-NA SONG 56

RUN, BABY, RUN 49

STRONG ENOUGH 60

ALL I WANNA DO

Words and Music by
SHERYL CROW, WYN COOPER, BILL BOTTRELL,
DAVID BAERWALD and KEVIN GILBERT

6

Bridge:

w/Rhy. Fig. 1 (Gtr. 2)

Chorus:

Gtr. 2

Cont. rhy. simile

Gtr. 1

All I Wanna Do – 6 – 3
0067B

8

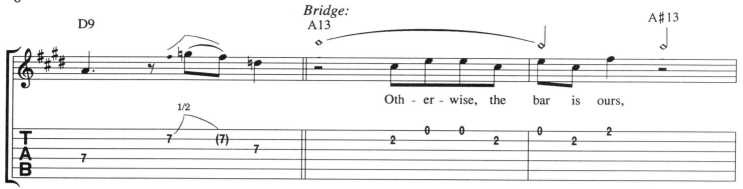

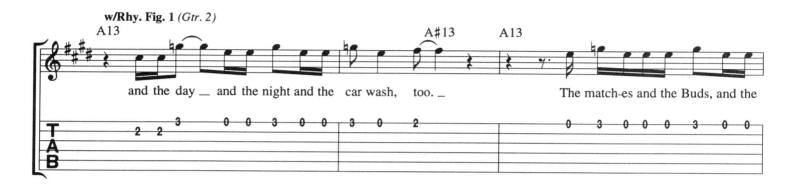

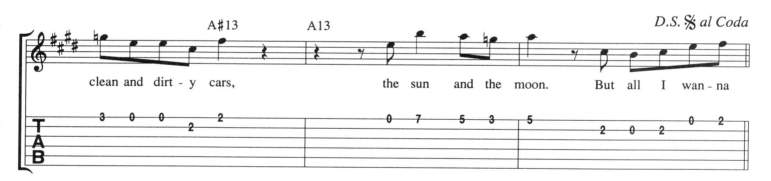

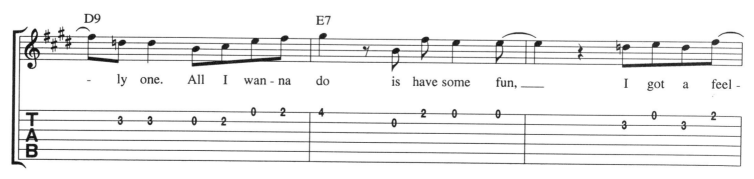

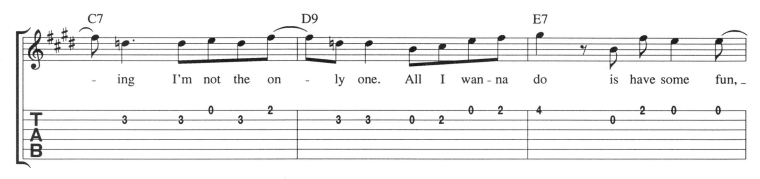

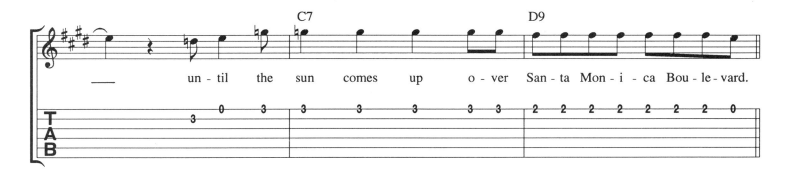

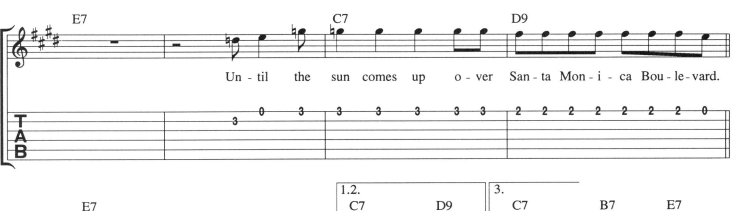

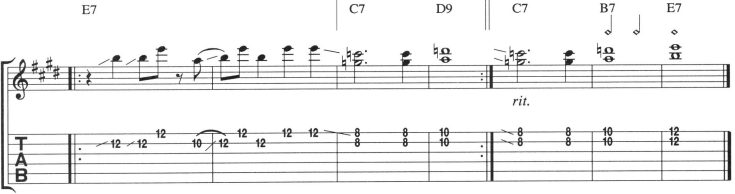

Verse 2:
I like a good beer buzz early in the morning,
And Billy likes to peel the labels from his bottles of Bud
And shreds them on the bar.
Then he lights every match in an oversized pack,
Letting each one burn down to his thick fingers
Before blowing and cursing them out.
And he's watching the Buds as they spin on the floor.
A happy couple enters the bar dancing dangerously close to one another.
The bartender looks up from his wants ads.
(To Chorus:)

CAN'T CRY ANYMORE

Words and Music by
SHERYL CROW and BILL BOTTRELL

Can't Cry Anymore – 4 – 1

0067B

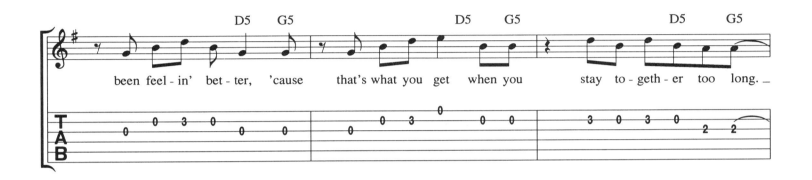

Can't Cry Anymore – 4 – 2
0067B

Verse 3:
And now I know that
Money comes in,
But the fact is (there's)
Not enough to pay my taxes.
And I can't cry anymore.
(To Chorus:)

Verse 4:
Well, gotta brother.
He's got real problems.
Heroin now,
There's just no stopping him tonight.
And I won't cry anymore.
(To Chorus:)

Verse 5:
Well, it could be worse.
I could've missed my calling.
Sometimes it hurts,
But when you read the writing on the wall,
Can't cry anymore.
(To Chorus:)

A CHANGE WOULD DO YOU GOOD

Words and Music by
SHERYL CROW, BRIAN MacLEOD and JEFF TROTT

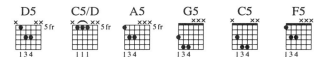

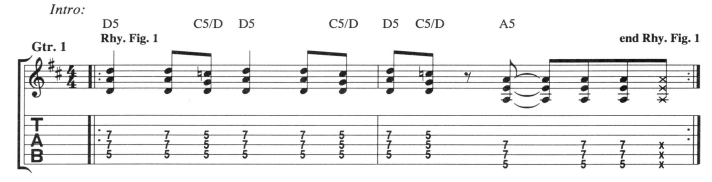

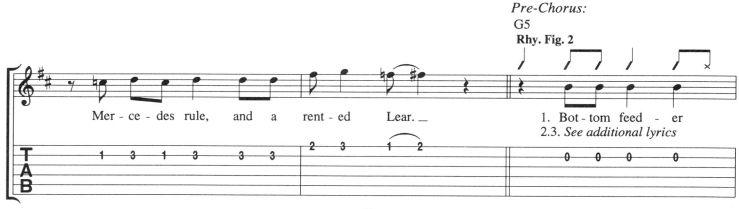

A Change Would Do You Good - 4 - 1
0067B

w/Rhy. Fig. 1 *(Gtr. 1) 4 times*

like to reach __ me, leave me a - lone. __ I think a change

would do you good. __ I think a

Repeat & fade

change would do you good. __

Verse 2:
God's little gift is on the rag.
Poster girl posing in a fashion mag.
Canine, feline, Jekyll and Hyde?
Wear your fake fur on the inside.

Pre-Chorus 2:
Queen of South Beach, aging blues.
Dinner's at six, wear your cement shoes.
I thought you were singing your heart out to me.
Your lips were syncing and now I see.
(To Chorus:)

Verse 3:
Chasing dragons with plastic swords.
Jack off Jimmy, everybody wants more.
Scully and Angel on the kitchen floor.
And I'm calling Buddy on the Ouiji board.

Pre-Chorus 3:
I've been thinking 'bout catching a train,
Leave my phone machine by the radar range.
"Hello, it's me, I'm not at home.
If you'd like to reach me, leave me alone."
(To Chorus:)

EVERYDAY IS A WINDING ROAD

Words and Music by
SHERYL CROW, BRIAN MacLEOD and JEFF TROTT

Everyday is a Winding Road – 6 – 1
0067B

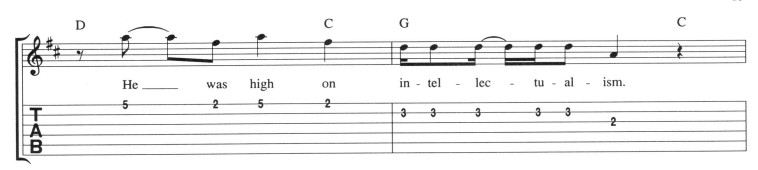

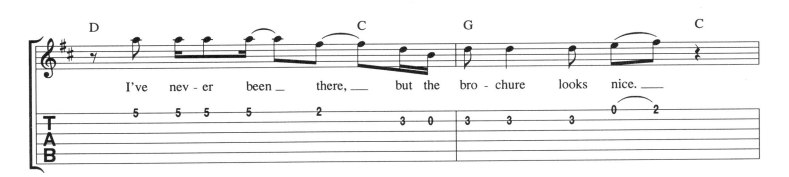

Pre-Chorus:

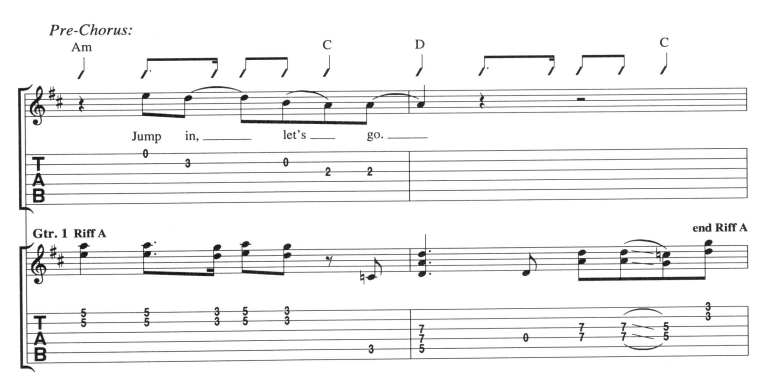

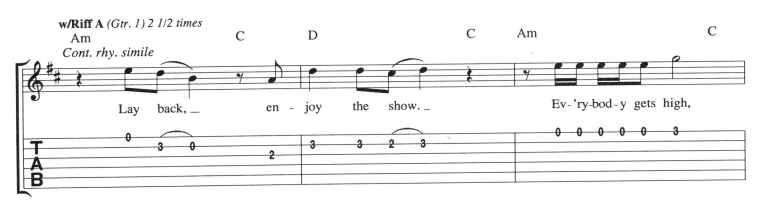

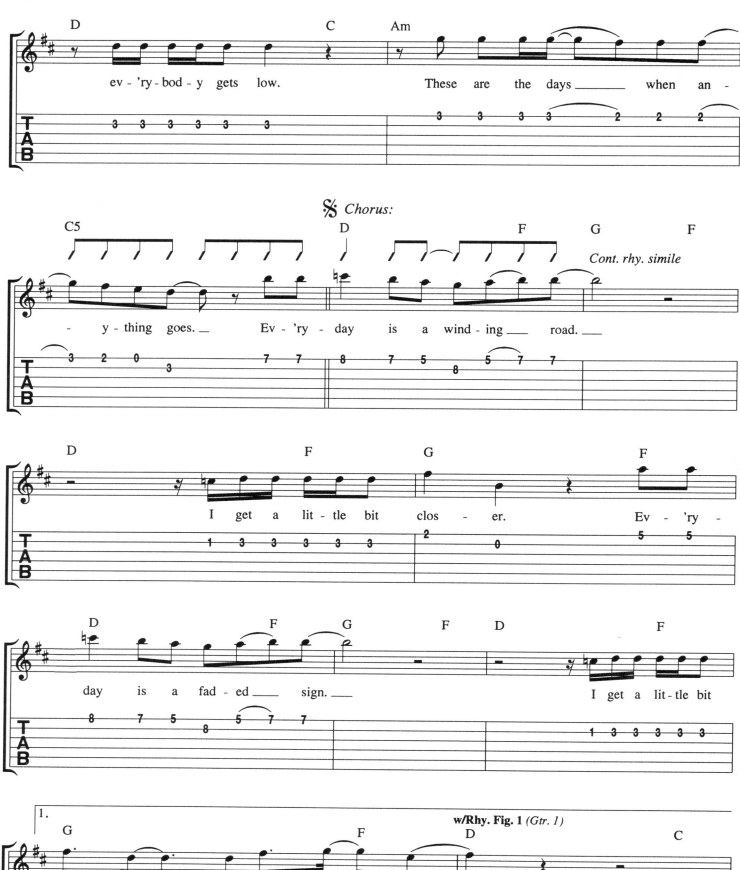

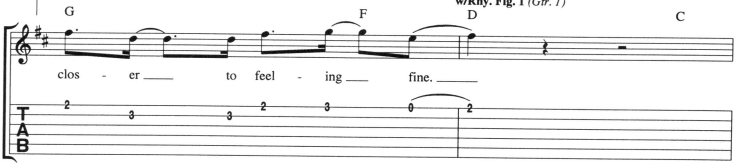

Everyday is a Winding Road – 6 – 3
0067B

Everyday is a Winding Road – 6 – 5
0067B

Verse 2:
He's got a daughter he calls Easter,
She was born on a Tuesday night.
I'm just wondering why I feel so all alone,
Why I'm a stranger in my own life.
(To Pre-Chorus:)

HARD TO MAKE A STAND

Words and Music by
SHERYL CROW, BILL BOTTRELL,
TODD WOLFE and ROY SCOTT BRYAN

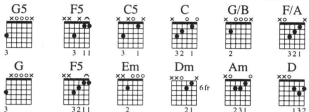

Moderately ♩ = 102

Intro:

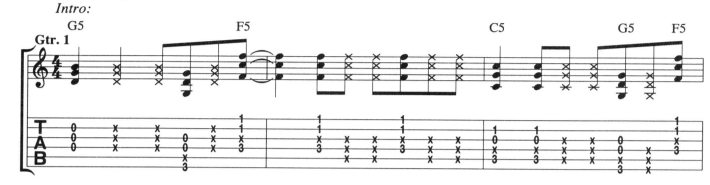

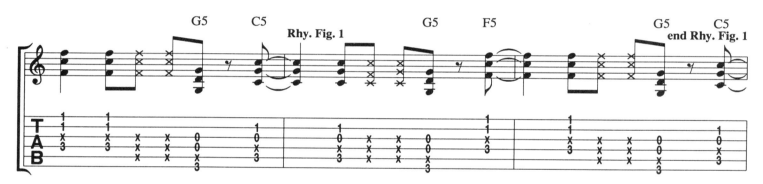

Verse:
w/Rhy. Fig. 1 *(Gtr. 1) 4 times, simile*

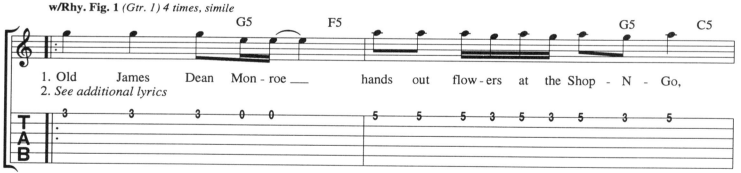

1. Old James Dean Mon-roe ___ hands out flow-ers at the Shop - N - Go,
2. *See additional lyrics*

hopes for mon-ey but all he gets ___ is fear. ___ And the

Hard to Make a Stand - 4 - 1
0067B

wind blows up his coat, ___ and this he scrib-bles on a per-fume note, "If

I'm not here, then you're ___ not here." ___ And he ___ says,

Pre-Chorus:

1. "Call _____ me Mis-cre-a-tion, I'm a ___ walk-ing cel-e-bra-tion." And it's
2. *See additional lyrics*

Gtr. 1
Rhy. Fig. 2

end Rhy. Fig. 2

%. **Chorus:**
  w/**Rhy. Fig. 1** *(Gtr. 1) 3 times, simile*

hard to make a stand. ___   Yeah.   And it's hard ___ to make a stand. ___

Hard to Make a Stand – 4 – 2
0067B

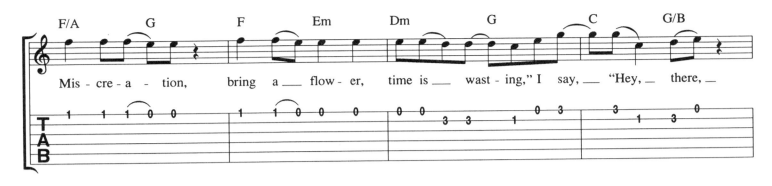

Mis - cre - a - tion, bring a __ flow - er, time is __ wast - ing," I say, __ "Hey, __ there, __

D.S. 𝄋 al Coda

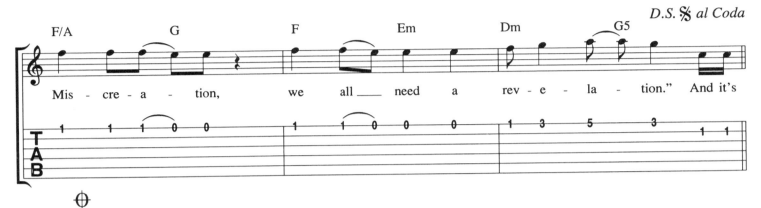

Mis - cre - a - tion, we all __ need a rev - e - la - tion." And it's

Coda

w/Rhy. Fig. 1 *(Gtr. 1) 2 times, simile*

__ to make a stand, __ oh, I think it's hard __ to make a stand. __

Repeat and fade

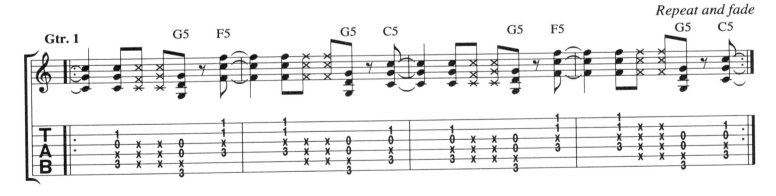

Verse 2:
My friend, o lawdy, went to take care of her own body,
And she got shot down in the road.
And she looked up before she went, said,
"This isn't really what I meant."
And the Daily News said, "Two With One Stone."

Pre-Chorus 2:
"Hey there, Miscreation,
Bring a flower,
Time is wasting."
(To Chorus:)

Hard to Make a Stand – 4 – 4
0067B

IF IT MAKES YOU HAPPY

Words and Music by
SHERYL CROW and JEFF TROTT

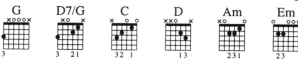

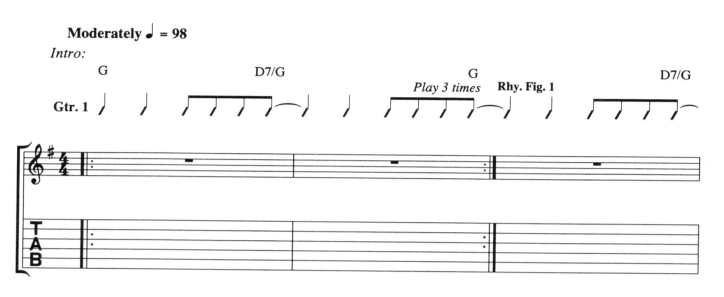

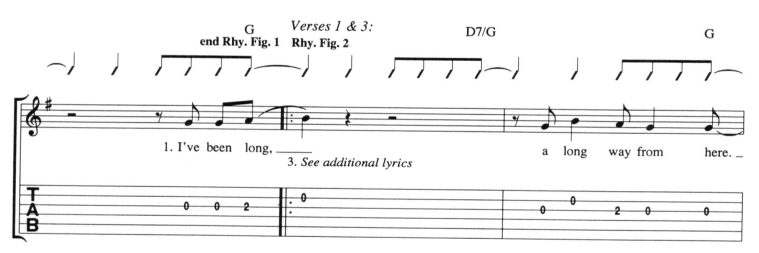

If it Makes You Happy – 5 – 1
0067B

If it Makes You Happy – 5 – 4
0067B

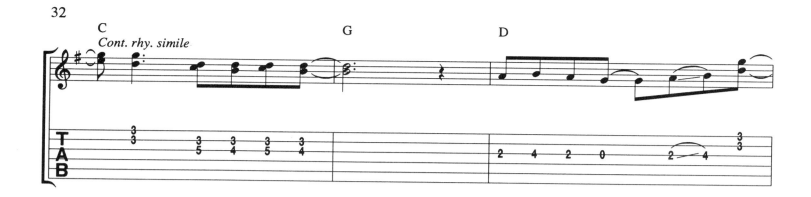

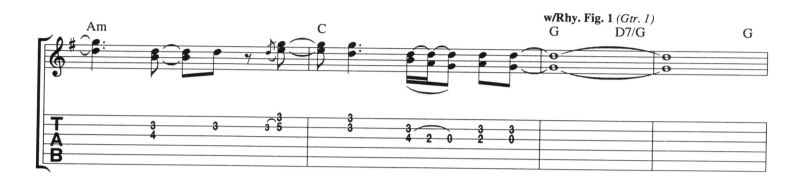

Verse 3:
You get down, real low down.
You listen to Coltrane, derail your own train.
Well, who hasn't been there before?

Verse 4:
I come 'round, around the hard way.
Bring your comics in bed, scrape the mold off the bread,
And serve you French toast again.

Pre-Chorus 2:
Well, okay, I still get stoned.
I'm not the kind of girl you'd take home.
(To Chorus:)

Verse 5:
We've been far, far away from here.
Put on a poncho, played for mosquitoes,
And everywhere in between.

Pre-Chorus 3:
Well, o.k., we get along.
So what if right now everything's wrong?
(To Chorus:)

LEAVING LAS VEGAS

Words and Music by
SHERYL CROW, BILL BOTTRELL, DAVID BAERWALD,
KEVIN GILBERT and DAVID RICKETTS

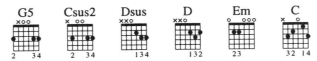

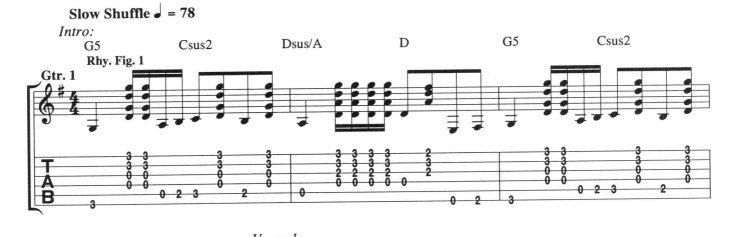

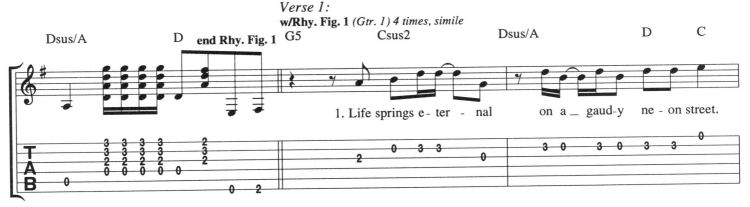

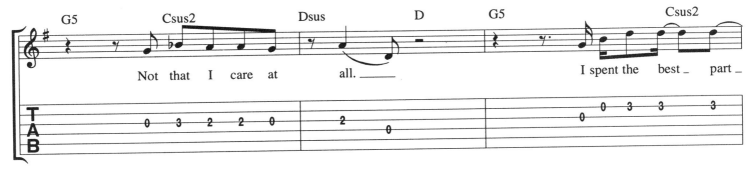

Leaving Las Vegas – 5 – 1
0067B

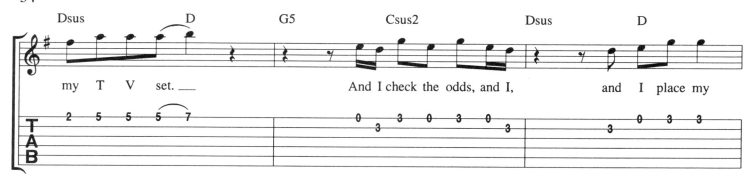

Chorus:
w/Rhy. Fig. 1 *(Gtr. 1) 3 times, simile*

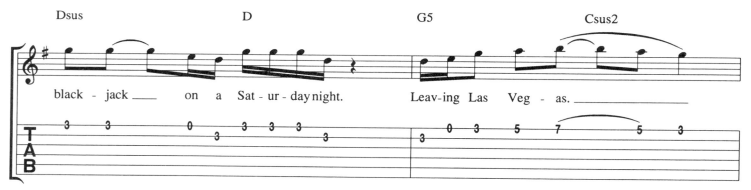

Verse 3:
Quit my job as a dancer
At the Lido des Girls,
Dealing blackjack until one or two.
Such a muddy line between
The things you want
And the things you have to do.
(To Chorus:)

LOVE IS A GOOD THING

Words and Music by
SHERYL CROW and TAD WADHAMS

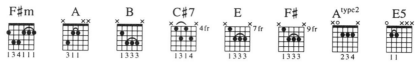

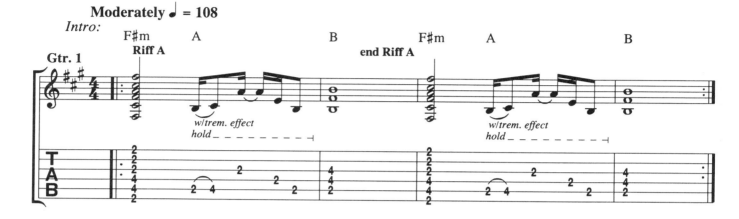

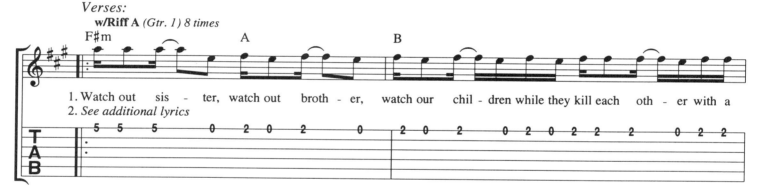

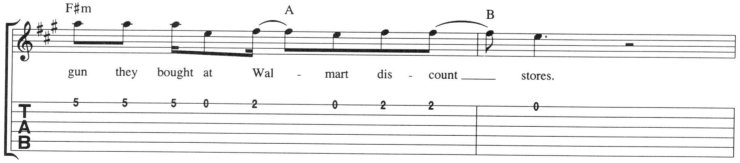

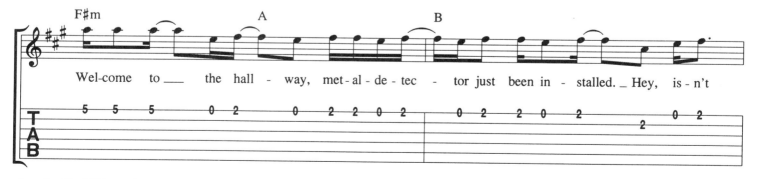

Love is a Good Thing – 6 – 1
0067B

Pre-Chorus:

C#7

Gtr. 1

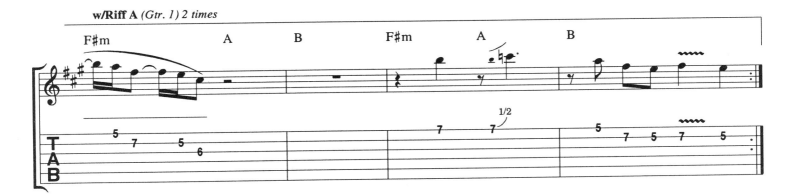

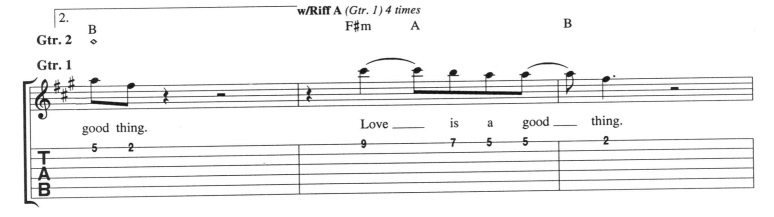

Love is a Good Thing – 6 – 4
0067B

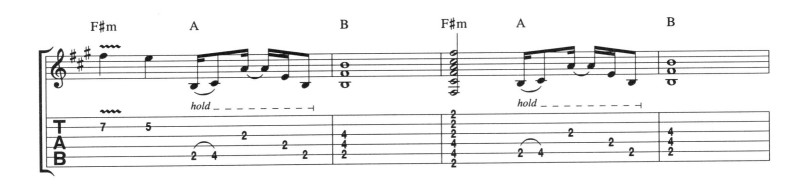

w/Riff A *(Gtr. 1) 2 times*

Repeat and fade

Verse 2:
Politicians on a mission, bring them up,
Bring them down for the good of the "system."
Well, we don't like the way you live your life.
I got one thing I must express,
We try our criminals in the press.
Justice is a faded light.
Mary, Mary, quite contrary, close your door now,
It's much to scary, and you might see
Something you wish you hadn't seen.
Out of sight, out of time, out of patience,
And I'm out of mind.
Gov'ner, tell me what does it mean?
(To Chorus:)

MAYBE ANGELS

Words and Music by
SHERYL CROW and BILL BOTTRELL

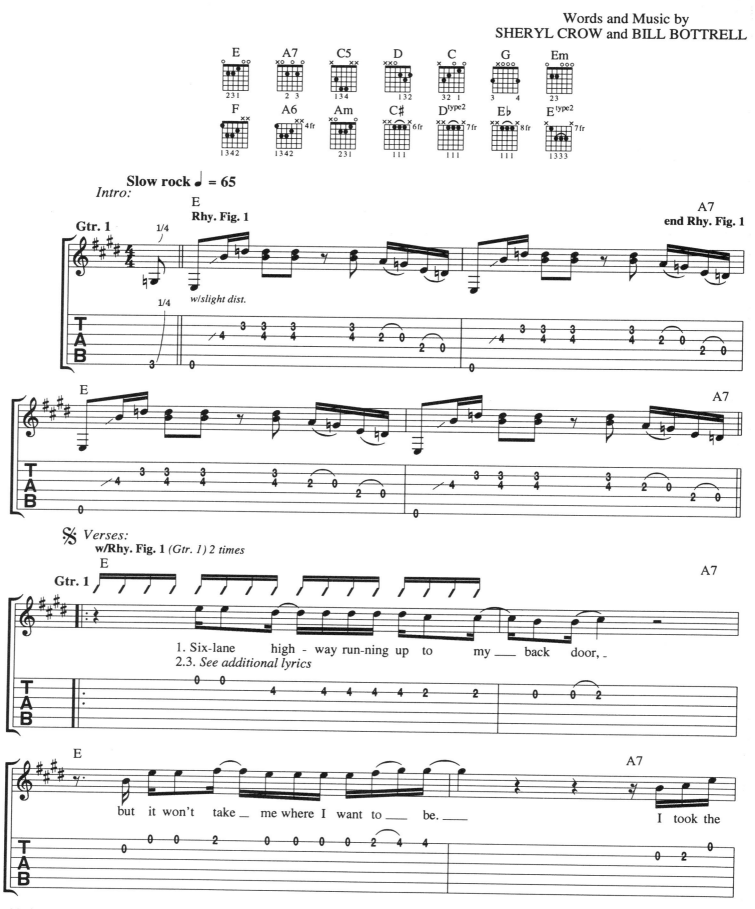

Maybe Angels – 5 – 1
0067B

I - Nine-ty-five down to Pen-sa-co-la, all I found _ was a bunch of ho-ly roll-ers.

They don't know _ noth-ing 'bout sav-ing me. ____ I

Chorus:

swear they're out _ there, I swear. I

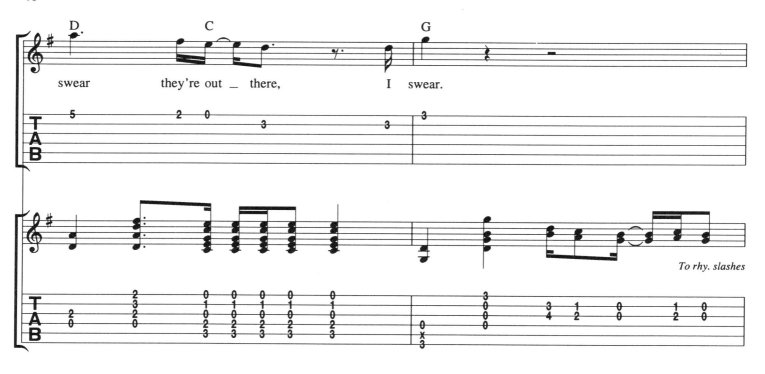

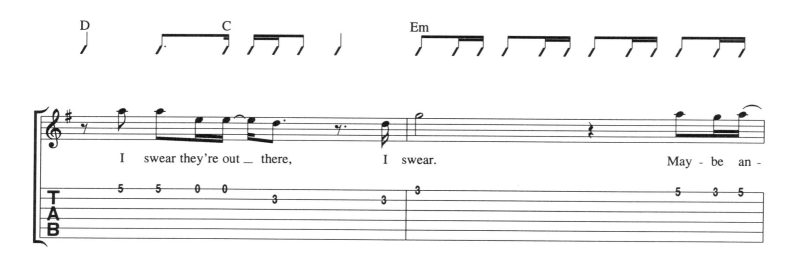

Verse 2:
Down here I feel like a citizen of nowhere.
My bag's all packed in case they ever come for me.
Got a hundred stories and tabloid lies.
Got witnesses to what the government denies.
So I'm headed down to Roswell to wait and see.
(To Chorus:)

Verse 3:
My sister, she says she knows Elvis.
She knows Jesus, John Lennon and Cobain personally.
Uh, uh, but I'm too wise to believe my eyes
'Cause all I've seen just terrifies me.
But I believe they're coming back for me.
(To Chorus:)

RUN, BABY, RUN

Words and Music by
SHERYL CROW, BILL BOTTRELL
and DAVID BAERWALD

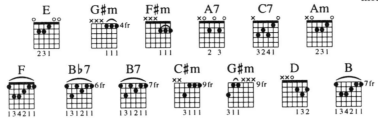

Moderately ♩. = 70

Verses:

1. She was born in No-vem-ber, nine-teen six-ty three.

Gtr. 1

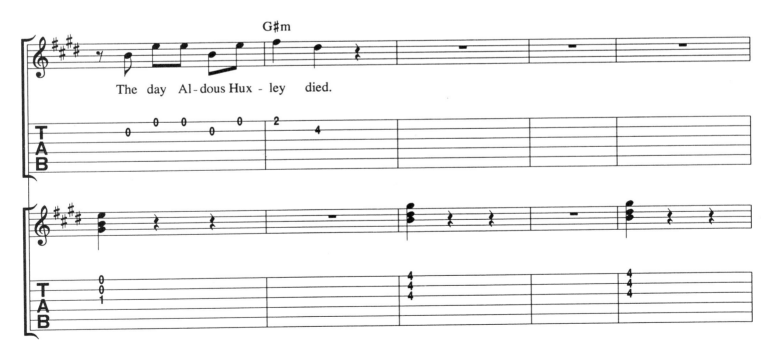

The day Al-dous Hux-ley died.

Run, Baby, Run – 7 – 1
0067B

50

52

Run, Baby, Run – 7 – 4
0067B

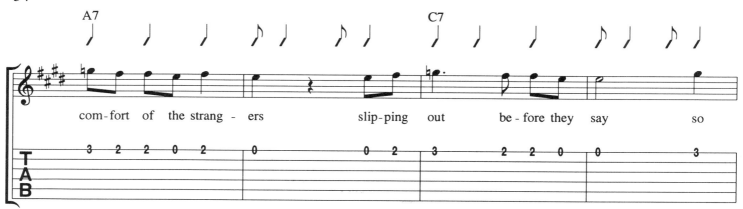

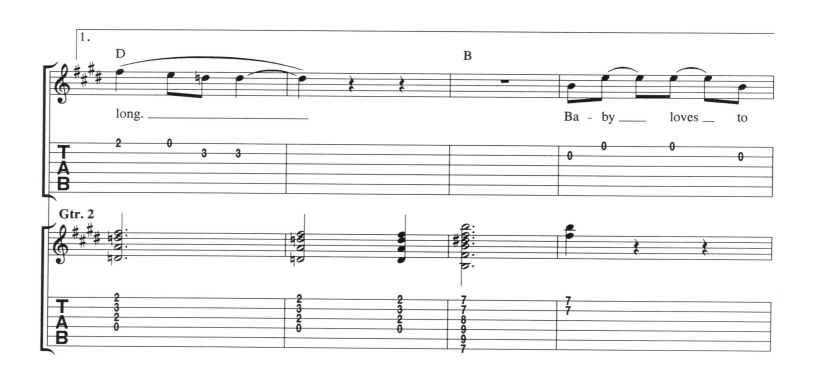

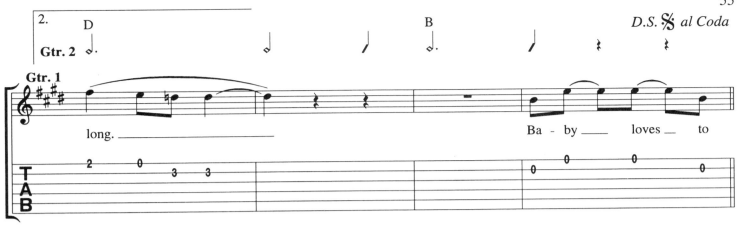

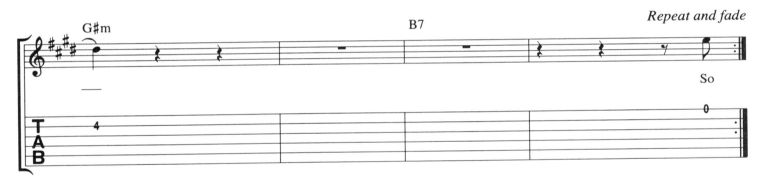

Verse 2:
She counts out all her money
In the taxi, on the way to meet her plane
And stares, hopeful, out the window
At the workers fighting through the pouring rain.
And she's searching through the stations
For an unfamiliar song.
And she's thinkin' 'bout the places
That she knows she still belongs.
She smiles the secret smile
That shows she knows exactly how to carry on.
(To Chorus:)

Bridge 2:
From their old familiar faces,
And their old familiar ways.
To the comfort of the strangers
Slippin' out before they say so long.
Baby loves to run.

Verse 3:
And she's searching through the stations
For an unfamiliar song.
And she pictures all the places
She knows she still belongs.
And smiles the secret smile
Because she knows exactly how to carry on.

THE NA-NA SONG

Words and Music by
SHERYL CROW, KEVIN GILBERT,
BRIAN MACLEOD, DAVID RICKETTS,
BILL BOTTRELL and DAVID BAERWALD

A5

Moderately slow ♩ = 80

Intro:

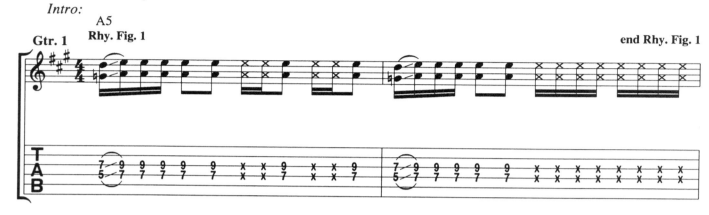

𝄋 *Verses 1 & 3:*

w/Rhy. Fig. 1 *(Gtr. 1) 4 times, simile*

1. Vid - e - o count down cy - ber - phal - lic op - tics. Prof - li - gate talk shows scroung - ing for a top - ic.
3. *See additional lyrics*

The Na-Na Song – 4 – 1
0067B

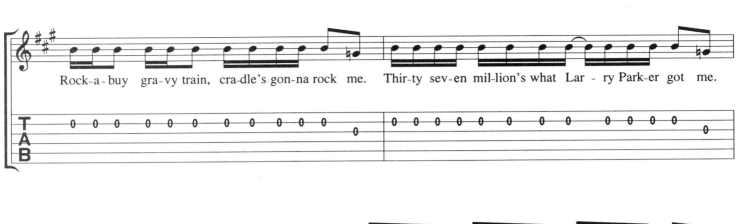

Rock-a-buy gra-vy train, cra-dle's gon-na rock me. Thir-ty sev-en mil-lion's what Lar-ry Park-er got me.

World War Four-teen my first So-ny. Bea-tles wrote the Ni-ke song and called it mac-a-ro-ni.

Bil-lie Jean, Bur-ger King, chau-vin-ist pig-pen. U. S. Ar-my on-ly wants a few straight men.

Chorus:
w/Rhy. Fig. 1 *(Gtr. 1) 2 times, simile*

To Coda ⊕

Na - na na - na na - na na - na na - na na - na.___

Verse 2:
w/Rhy. Fig. 1 *(Gtr. 1) 5 times, simile*

2. Pan-a-flex, so-lo-flex, Gen-u-flect Pope, what the world needs now is ba - bies, guns and hope.

The Na-Na Song – 4 – 2
0067B

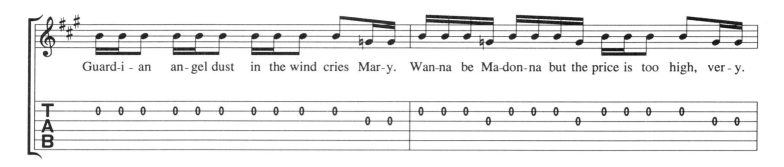

Guard-i - an an-gel dust in the wind cries Mar-y. Wan-na be Ma-don-na but the price is too high, ver-y.

Per-fect rhy-thm Na-zis in the pa-gan rhy-thm na-tion. Ev-'ry bod-y's e-qual in the glow of ra-di-a-tion. Got-ta

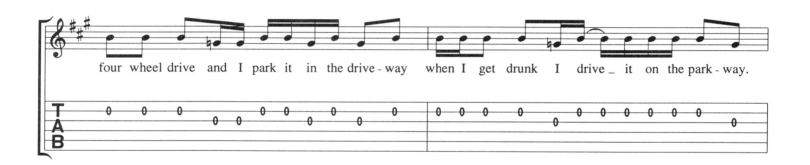

four wheel drive and I park it in the drive-way when I get drunk I drive _ it on the park-way.

Got to get a T V set for my car. To - night's the bat - tle of the Net-work Stars.

w/Rhy. Fig. 1 *(Gtr. 1) 4 times, simile*

Na - na na - na na - na na - na na - na na - na. ____

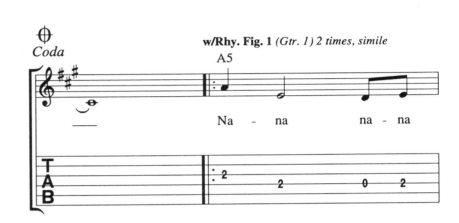

Verse 3:
Saniflush Bud-Bowl makin' me sick,
'Cause anybody in a helmet looks just like a dick.
Steely Dan Rather be a hammer than a nail.
The Serbs, the Poles and the check's in the mail.
Eat, sleep, die, lie record label.
G. Gordon Liddy under the table, table, table.
Clarence Thomas organ grinder Frank Dileo's dong.
Maybe if I let him I'd've had a hit song.
(To Chorus:)

STRONG ENOUGH

Words and Music by
SHERYL CROW, KEVIN GILBERT, BRIAN MACLEOD,
DAVID RICKETTS, BILL BOTTRELL and DAVID BAERWALD

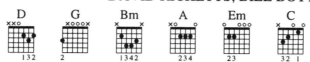

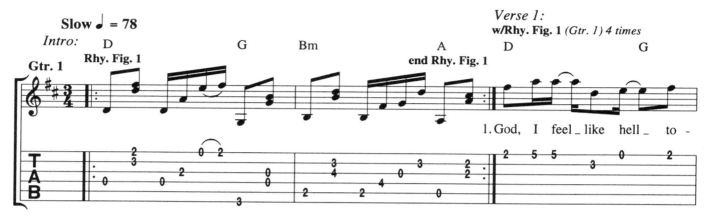

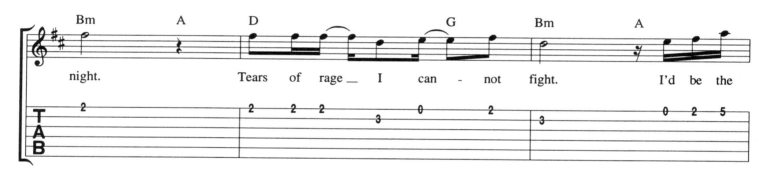

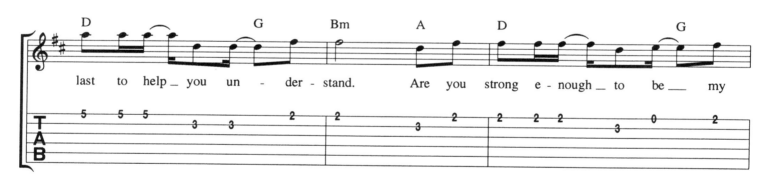

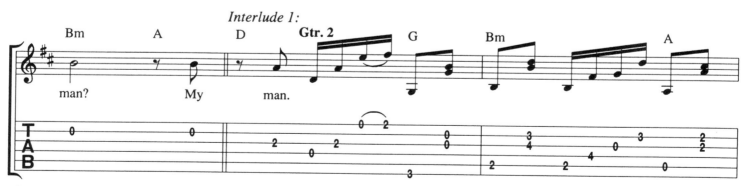

Strong Enough – 4 – 1
0067B

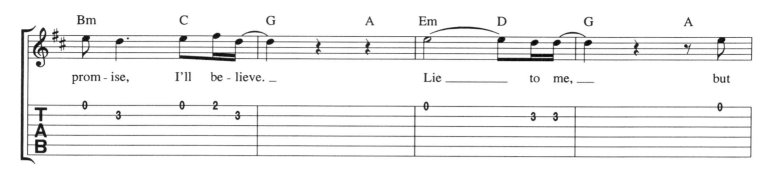

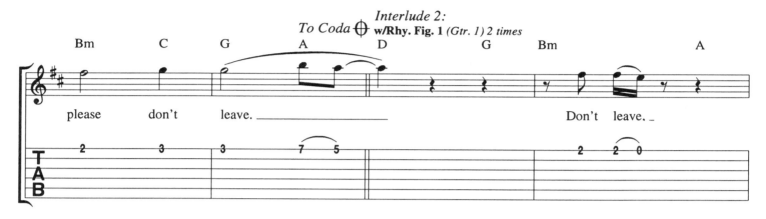

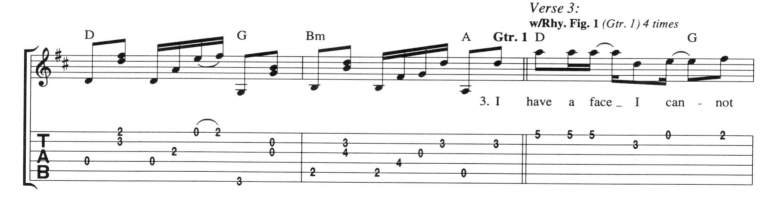

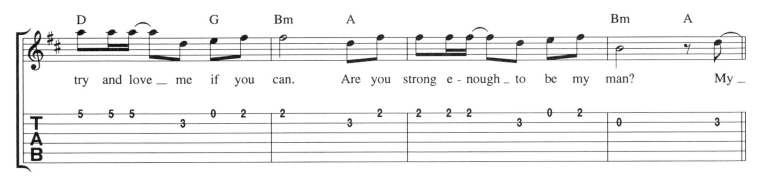

w/Rhy. Fig. 1 *(Gtr. 1) 4 times*

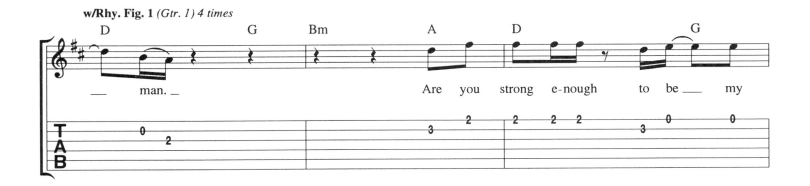

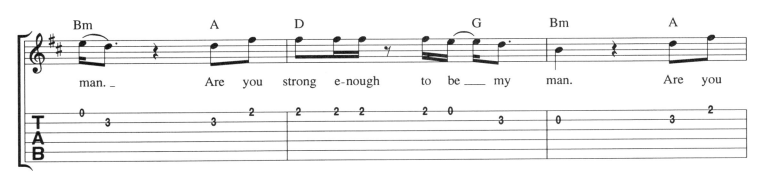

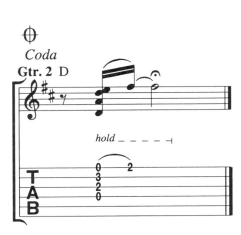

Verse 4:
When I've shown you that I just don't care,
When I'm throwing punches in the air,
When I'm broken down and I can't stand,
Will you be man enough to be my man?
(To Chorus:)

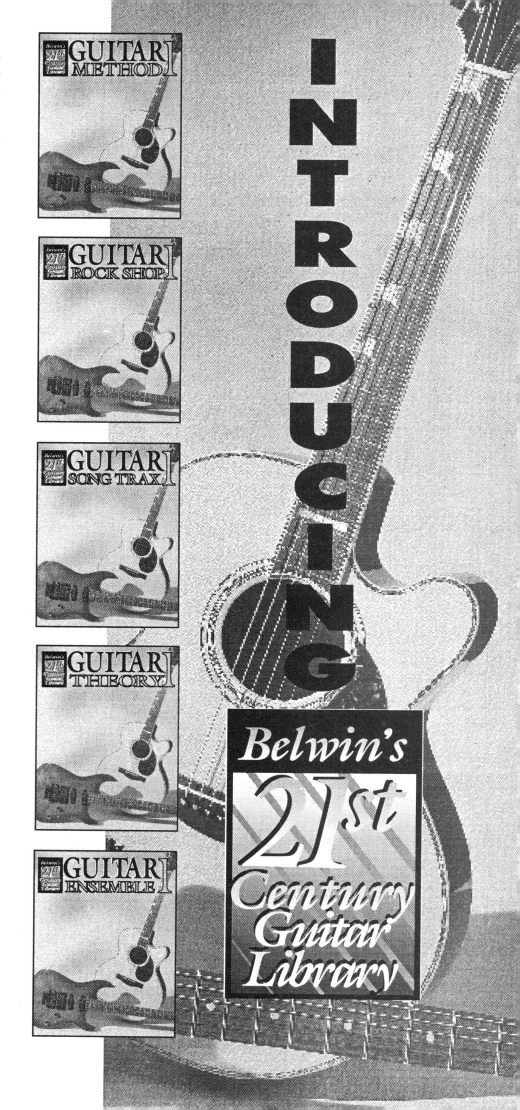

Most guitarists have — or want to have — one foot in the traditional scene and one foot in the contemporary scene. This method addresses both styles with charismatic flair AND solid pedagogy.

Most teachers want to teach according to the needs of individual students. With all the options in Belwin's 21st Century Guitar Library, teachers have it all!

classical ■ *rock* ■ *pop* ■ *folk*
lead guitar ■ *rock rhythm*
standard notation and tablature
accompaniments
blues and rock riffs ■ *power chords*
lead scales
note reading ■ *creativity*
lesson plans ■ *performance tips*
fretboard understanding
musicianship

Available from your favorite music dealer:

LEVEL 1
(EL 03842) Guitar Method 1
(EL 03842AT) Guitar Method 1 w/Cassette
(EL 03842CD) Guitar Method 1 w/CD
(EL 03851AT) Guitar Rock Shop 1 w/Cassette
(EL 03851CD) Guitar Rock Shop 1 w/CD
(EL 03845) Guitar Theory 1
(EL 03848AT) Guitar Song Trax 1 w/Cassette
(EL 03848CD) Guitar Song Trax 1 w/CD
(EL 03955S) Guitar Ensemble Student Book 1
(EL 03955AT) Guitar Ensemble Score Book 1
   w/Cassette
(EL 03955CD) Guitar Ensemble Score Book 1
   w/CD
(EL 03960) Guitar Teacher Edition 1

LEVEL 2
(EL 03843) Guitar Method 2
(EL 03843AT) Guitar Method 2 w/Cassette
(EL 03843CD) Guitar Method 2 w/CD
(EL 03852AT) Guitar Rock Shop 2 w/Cassette
(EL 03852CD) Guitar Rock Shop 2 w/CD
(EL 03846) Guitar Theory 2
(EL 03849AT) Guitar Song Trax 2 w/Cassette
(EL 03849CD) Guitar Song Trax 2 w/CD
(EL 03957S) Guitar Ensemble Student Book 2
(EL 03957AT) Guitar Ensemble Score Book 2
   w/Cassette
(EL 03957CD) Guitar Ensemble Score Book 2
   w/CD
(EL 03961) Guitar Teacher Edition 2

Level 3 coming soon

INTRODUCING

Belwin's
21st
Century
Guitar
Library